WITHDRAWN

I am
Donald Trump

I am Donald Trump

By Felicia S. Hudson

Illustrated by Sophia Ian

I am Donald Trump

A collection of biographies from the *Who Am I Series* an OPEN UNIVERSAL LIBRARY biography

PUBLISHED 2017
by Open Universal Library.
First Edition.

ISBN: 978-1543295757

Also by Open Universal Library:

I am Barack Obama
I am Muhammad Ali
I am Albert Einstien
I am Justin Bieber
I am Walt Disney
I am LeBron James
I am Leonardo Da Vinci

All rights reserved; no part of this book may be reproduced by any means, electronic, mechanical, photocopying or otherwise, without the prior permission of the publisher.

Copyrights © 2017
Cover and design layout by Alisa Longoria
Written and reproduced by Felicia S. Hudson Copyrights © Open Universal Library
Illustrations by Sophia Ian Copyrights © Open Universal Library

www.openuiniversallibrary.com

Contents

Prologue 6

Chapter 1 — The Trump Family 9

Chapter 2 — The Trump Tower 19

Chapter 3 — Trump Associations 27

Chapter 4 — The Trump Empire 35

Chapter 5 — The Trump Welfare Works 45

Chapter 6 — Trump's Political Ambitions 53

Chapter 7 — Trump's Presidential Campaign 62

Chapter 8 — The Trump Mansion 72

Chapter 9 — Trump's Success 80

Chapter 10 — The Trump Presidency 88

Timeline 98

Bibliography 100

Prologue

Donald Trump is a household name these days. This American businessman, politician and President-elect of the United States of America, will take office early in 2017.

70 year-old Trump is the oldest President-elect in U.S. history, and he is also the wealthiest. He advocates a non-interventionist approach to foreign policy. Trump identifies himself as

conservative and his ideology is described as populist, protectionist and nationalist.

However, his victory was not welcomed by all Americans. There were many public protests to some of his policies and comments he made during his campaign. Trump reacted with a Tweet saying that he 'loves their passion for the country'.

An interesting fact about Trump, is that he is very healthy. According to him he has never smoked cigarettes or marijuana, or consumed other drugs. He does not drink alcohol either. That explains why he opposes legalizing recreational

marijuana but supports legalizing marijuana for medical uses.

Donald Trump is a businessman, family man, politician and TV personality. Read more about this father of five and grandfather of eight's childhood, private life and how he came from being the child of a real estate agent to one of the world's richest people.

You will see that he had a full, controversial life with many ups and downs, but Trump doesn't give up easily. Let's see why...

Chapter 1
The Trump Family

Donald John Trump, the fourth of five children of Fred Trump and Mary MacLeod Trump, was born in Queens, New York on June 14, 1946. Donald had two sisters, Maryanne Trump and Elizabeth, and two brothers Fred Jr. and Robert S. Trump.

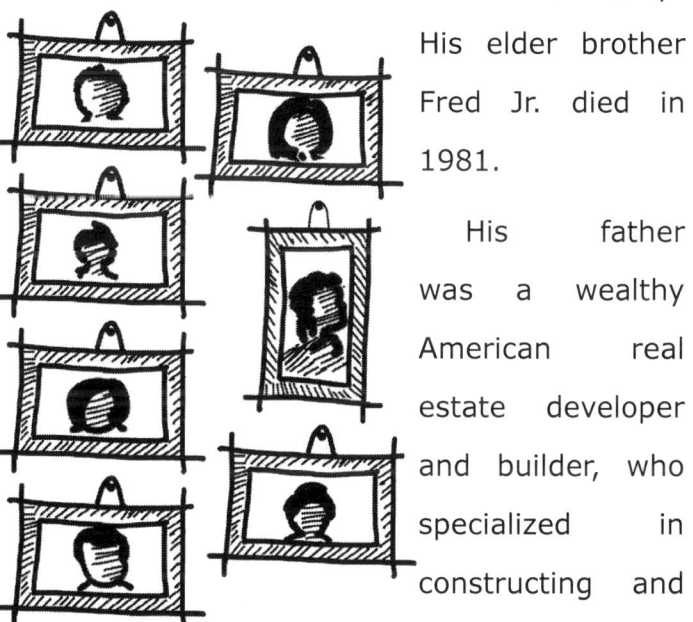

His elder brother Fred Jr. died in 1981.

His father was a wealthy American real estate developer and builder, who specialized in constructing and operating middle-income apartments. He met Mary Trump in New York and started living in Queens after their marriage in 1936. The Trump family is a famous German and German-American family of Lutheran origins (a branch of Protestant Christianity identifying with the theology of Martin Luther). Many of its family members moved to the United States in the 19th

century. One of the most prominent branches of the family's members is Donald Trump's family; the 45th elected president of the United States of America.

Donald Trump received his early education from The Kew-Forest School, which he left at

the age of 13 to enrol into the New York Military Academy (NYMA) in Cornwall, New York. He was an assertive child, so one of the main aims of his parents was to help him channel his energy in a positive manner, through the discipline of military school. There he rose to become a star

athlete and student leader. He completed grade eight and high school from NYMA and attained the rank of a captain by the time he graduated. In August 1964, he went to attend the Fordham University in the Bronx for two years until he then transferred to the Wharton School at the prestigious University of Pennsylvania. This was one of the few schools in the United States to have a real estate studies department. While obtaining his B.S in economics from Wharton School, Trump started working at the family's company, named

after his paternal grandmother, Elizabeth Trump & Son. He graduated from Wharton in May 1968.

Nine years after his graduation, Trump married his first wife, Ivana Marie Trump; a Czech-American businesswoman, author, socialite and fashion model on April 7, 1977. The couple had three children: a son Donald Jr. (born

on December 31, 1977) then a daughter Ivanka, (born on October 30, 1981). The youngest son, Eric, was born on January 6, 1984. The couple divorced in 1990.

Trump's second marriage with actress Marla Maples took place on the December 20, 1993, about two months after the birth of their first daughter Tiffany on October 14 of that year. She was named after the famous retailer 'Tiffany & Company'. However, Tiffany was raised by her mother in California after her parents' divorce in June 1999.

Trump is a hard working businessman who claims to love his work and believes his first two wives couldn't compete with his affection for working. On January 22, 2005, Trump married his third wife, Melania Klauss, a Slovene model whom he had been in a relationship with since 1998. The marriage was a grand event celebrated at West Palm Beach in Florida. On March 20, 2005, Melania gave birth to their son, Barron Trump.

Trump is a follower of Presbyterianism, a branch of Protestantism consisting of reformed traditions. He is said to have attended Sunday school and otherwise at a Presbyterian Church since childhood in Queens.

Donald Trump, the Republican Party nominee, was able to defeat the Democratic Party nominee Hillary Clinton, in the 58th quadrennial American Presidential elections held on November 8, 2016, making him the 45th elected president of the U.S. His opponent Hillary Clinton was not only the former Secretary of State and Senate, but also the first woman to be nominated by a major party to stand for president of the U.S. Despite winning the plurality of votes, Clinton lost and Trump is expected to take office as the 45th elected president of the U.S. on January 20, 2017.

Chapter 2
The Trump Tower

Influenced by his father, Trump decided to take on a career in real estate development at an early stage of his life, but with greater plans. He started working at Elizabeth Trump & Son while he was only a student. After graduating with more knowledge of economic models and business markets, Trump was able to convince

his father to let him make liberal use of loans for the expansion of the company's holding of rental housing, despite narrow profit margins.

In 1971 he moved in to a studio apartment in Manhattan. By this time, he had earned the family's trust and was given control of the company which he renamed the Trump Organization and became the president of the organization in 1973. The organization focused on middle class rental housing in the New York

City boroughs of Brooklyn, Queens and Staten Island. Fred and Donald Trump claimed to be screening out people who wanted to rent out apartments aimed at lower incomes. However, his business practices were called into question when they were accused by the Justice Department of discriminating against potential black tenants. Although the Trumps never agreed to admit responsibility for the allegations, they were made to sign an agreement in 1975 under which

the Trump Company had to train its employees according to the Fair Housing Act and inform the community about its unbiased housing practices. Trump wrote about the resolution of the case in his 1987 memoir *Art of the Deal*: "In the end, the government couldn't prove its case, and we ended up taking a minor settlement without admitting any guilt."

He became deeply involved in the project and with a $500,000 investment, turned a 1200 unit apartment complex in Cincinnati with a 66 percent vacancy rate to 100 percent occupancy within two years. He evaluated economic opportunities available in the city and became involved in large

EQUAL HOUSING OPPORTUNITY

building projects after making some important connections with influential people. He knew the city was undergoing a severe fiscal crisis and any new investment negotiations would be welcomed. Things went just as planned. He was allowed tax concessions from the city and started renovating and building hotel complexes and apartment towers. With the use of attractive architectural designs, he won public recognition. His first big deal in Manhattan, was the remodelling of the older Commodore Hotel in 1978, which was

mainly funded by a $70 million construction loan, jointly guaranteed by Fred Trump and the Hyatt Hotel Chain. When the hotel, renamed the Grand Hyatt, opened in 1980, it was instantly popular and proved an economic success, making Donald Trump the city's most well known developer.

His obsession with Tiffany & Company didn't quite end with the naming of his daughter. In 1979, he leased a site as the location for the now world-renowned Fifth Avenue skyscraper; the Trump Tower, adjacent to Tiffany & Company.

The monumental $200-million apartment-retail complex was designed by the famous architect Der Scutt. The Trump Tower, a 58-story building, featured a six-story atrium and an 80-foot tall waterfall and was opened in 1983.

Trump Tower marked the first milestone to the beginning of the gigantic Trump Empire, which would continue in the years to come. The tower housed Donald Trump's penthouse condominium residence, the headquarters of the Trump Organization and a fully functional television studio set which was also the set for the NBC television show 'The Apprentice'. The aesthetically built tower brought Trump national attention.

Chapter 3
Trump Associations

Donald Trump made many other remarkable associations with people, companies and activities around the world. His popularity began to grow after the inauguration of the Trump Tower and continued rising when he made a brief foray into sports, purchasing the New Jersey Generals in

1983. They played in the U.S Football League but unfortunately lasted (like the entire league) for only two seasons.

Similarly, in 1996, he was able to gain ownership of the Miss Universe Organization through a partnership with NBC, which produces the Miss Universe, Miss USA and Miss Team USA pageants and owned part of it until 2015. By September 2015, Trump had become the sole owner of the Miss Universe Organization by purchasing NBC's stake. However, some controversies arose during

his tenure of the organization. Once regarding the winning contestant's profile credibility and again in 2012, when the show was claimed to have been rigged. However, Trump won against the claim through arbitration.

After his father's death in 1999, Trump and his siblings received equal portions of his father's highly valued estate. Following this, he completed the Trump World Tower; the 72 storey residential tower across from the United Nations headquarters and continued to purchase numerous land spaces of Manhattan's prime real estate.

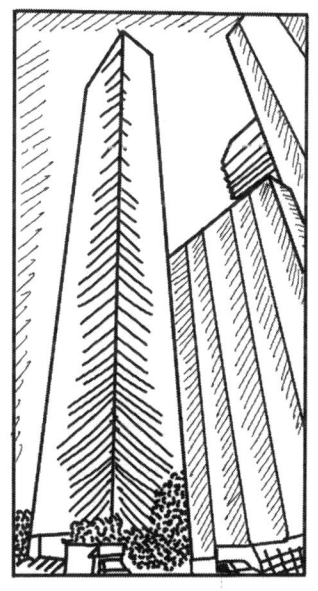

He also made a debut in the world of professional boxing, when he appeared on Wrestle Mania 23 in a match called "The Battle

of the Billionaires". He was in the Bobby Lashley's corner, while Vince McMahon was in the corner of Lashley's opponent, Umaga with Stone Cold Steve Austin as the special guest referee. They made a deal that either Trump or McMahon would shave their head if their competitor lost. McMahon lost his hair when Umaga was defeated. Being a WWE fan, Trump has been an active participant of several shows and hosted two Wrestle Mania events at the Trump Plaza.

The idea of running for president occurred to him several times in 1988, 2004 and particularly in 2012. On October 7, 1999, Trump announced the formation of an exploratory committee to inform his decision, of whether or not to seek the Reform Party's nomination for the presidential race of 2000. However, after poor support during the California primary, Trump withdrew his candidacy. But his political stance still remained popular in many areas, especially California and

Michigan. Other than the Reform Party, he has had several different party affiliations over the years.

In 1989, Trump had bought an East Coast air shuttle service from American Airlines comprising of a fleet of Boeing 727 airplanes to form the *Trump Shuttle* air service. But due to the unfortunate deaths of three Trump casino executives in a helicopter crash, the service was later shut down.

In 1999, the Trump Model Management agency was founded by Trump in Lower Manhattan. The company brought around 250 foreign fashion models into the fashion industry of the United States.

In 2004 Trump took advantage of his high-profile persona and became the executive producer and host of the NBC reality series *The Apprentice*, in which contestants competed for a management position within the Trump Organization. The show was an instant hit and Trump's television catchphrase "You're fired", which he used to eliminate contestants from the game, became one of the most popular television catchphrases of all time. The success of the show resulted in numerous spin-offs, including *The Celebrity Apprentice* that showcased well-known figures as contestants. Trump is said to have been paid millions of dollars for the 14 seasons he hosted. He also earned himself a star on the Hollywood Walk of Fame in 2007, for his contribution to 'The Apprentice'. His association with the show ended in 2015.

Chapter 4
The Trump Empire

Completion of the Trump Tower in the heart of New York, was the first milestone achieved towards the building of the Trump Empire. With his hard work and dedication, Donald Trump was able to bring the business up a notch. Month after

month, he was signing new contracts, setting conditions, making amendments and was able to take the family business to where it now stands.

However, despite his businesses going bankrupt several times, Trump knew his way around bankruptcy laws and was able to avoid going bankrupt.

Soon after the Hyatt project, Trump started investigating other profitable business, and investigated the casino gambling business, which was approved in New Jersey in 1977. By 1980

he had bought a property in Atlantic City. Soon Trump and his brother Robert had obtained a gambling licence, permit and financing through the Holiday Inn Corporation, the parent company of Harrah's casino hotels. The partnership lead to the opening of the $250 million complex in 1984 as Harrah's at Trump Plaza. This was later renamed as the Trump Plaza Hotel and Casino after Trump bought out Holiday Inn. Trump also purchased the Hilton Hotels Casino in Atlantic City, after they failed to obtain a gambling license

and renamed the $320 million complex the Trump Castle.

Later, while it was under construction, he was able to acquire the largest hotel-casino in the world, the Taj Mahal in Atlantic City, which opened in 1990. However, it was closed down in 2016 due to multiple bankruptcies and labor strikes.

In 1985, the same year he bought the Mar-a-Lago estate in Palm Beach Florida, he purchased

76 acres on the West Side of Manhattan for $88 million. He wanted it in order to build a complex called Television City, which was to consist of a dozen skyscrapers, a mall and a riverfront park. The huge development was to invite television production and feature the world's tallest building. But community opposition and a long city-approval process delayed commencement of construction on the project. In 1988, he acquired

the Plaza Hotel for $407 million and spent $50 million refurbishing it.

However, his decline in the real estate market began in 1990, resulting in a reduction of income and value of Trump's Empire. Despite Trump's own net worth of $1.5 billion at that time, his organization required a massive infusion of loans due to his assets' investigated debt of around $50 million. Trump started defaulting on loans ever

since the failing of the Air Shuttle Project and lead to the termination of the venture in 1992.

But with a good understanding of economic models and efficient business strategies, Trump was able to climb his way back up. By 1997, he claimed to have reached the zenith of more than $2 billion from an estimated deficit of $900 million. His challenging ability was proven again, when he took over the repairs of the Wollman

Rink in Central Park, built in 1955. Repairs began in 1980 by a general contractor unconnected to Trump, with an expected 2 $\frac{1}{2}$-year construction schedule, but it was not completed by 1986. After Trump took over the project, he completed it in three months for $1.95 million, which was $750,000 less than the initial budget, and then operated the rink for one year with all profits going to charity in exchange for the rink's concession rights.

His empire experienced about six bankruptcies between 1990 and 2009, mainly resulting from

his casinos; the Taj Mahal, the Plaza Hotel, the Trump Castle Casino, the Trump Hotel and Casino Resorts and Trump Entertainment Resorts.

By 2000, they were back in business, making headlines yet again. In 1996, Trump acquired and renovated an old office building on Wall Street in Manhattan, turning it into the seventy-storey Trump Building at 40 Wall Street. By 2001, the Trump World Tower was completed and Trump also began construction on Trump Place, a multi-building development along the Hudson River. He continued to own commercial space in Trump International Hotel and Tower, a 44-story hotel and condominium tower on Columbus Circle, which he acquired in 1996, as well as owning millions of square feet of other prime Manhattan real estate. The former Hotel Delmonico in Manhattan in 2002 was also acquired and re-opened with 35 stories of luxury condominiums in 2004, called the Trump Park Avenue.

Chapter 5
The Trump Welfare Works

Trump: The Art of the Deal, was the first memoir-come-business model advisory book, written by Tony Schwartz and Donald Trump in 1987. The book tells of Trump's childhood and early life and the birth and growth of the Trump organization. It also relates the development of the Grand Hyatt Hotel and the establishment of Trump Tower. The book reveals his 11-step success formula for business entrepreneurs. Since the publication of the book by Random House in 1987, it has been translated into various languages.

Trump's contribution to society was not limited to economic development. He also played a key

role in the development of the educational and welfare sectors.

The Trump University, founded in 2004 by Donald Trump and his associates, specialized in running a real estate training program from 2005 to 2010. However, it wasn't an accredited university, it did not offer a degree or grades. It did however, claim to educate anyone well enough to turn them into a successful real estate investor. The company's original business plan focused on online education but it quickly expanded into

live, in-person instruction as well. They offered classes in rented spaces like hotel ballrooms and claimed to have chosen instructors through highly selective processes. However, despite a positive number of enrolments in their programs, the company was subject to lawsuits in federal court for falsely claiming itself a university when it wasn't actually chartered as one, and also for teaching misleading marketing practices.

In June 2010, 'Trump University' changed its name to 'The Trump Entrepreneur Initiative'. On November 18, 2016 it was reported that Trump agreed to pay $25 million to settle the two class-action lawsuits and the New York suit against him. Of the $25 million, $21 million will go to the

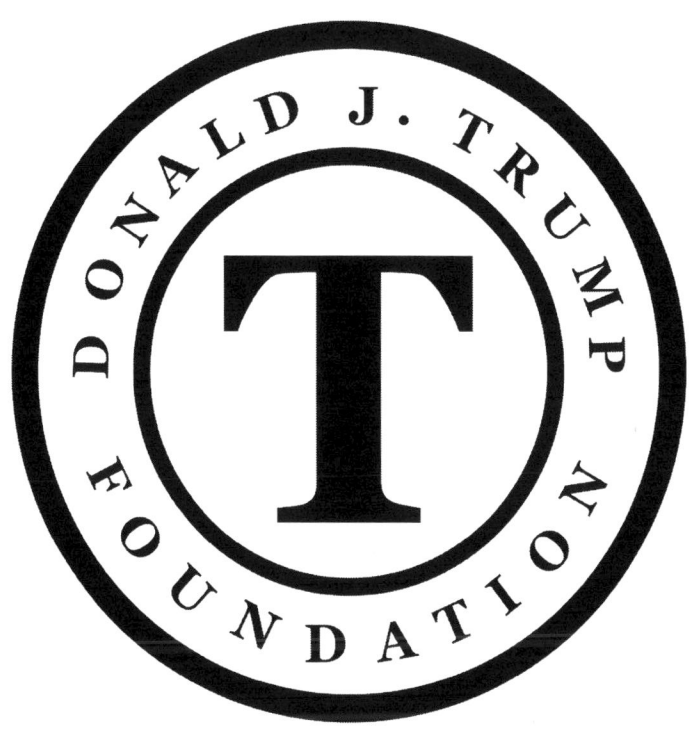

participants in the class-action suits, $3 million will go to New Yorkers not covered by the class-action suits, and a penalty of up to $1 million will be assessed by the state of New York for running an unlicensed university.

However, this was not the only contribution Trump made to the educational sector. A travelling lecture series was also founded in 2005 and was able to put on 120 seminars in 30 cities across the country. The seminar series was owned by Irene and Mike Milin, separately owned from the Trump University but with overlapping operations.

In 1988, the Donald J. Trump Foundation was founded as a private foundation. It grants money to tax-exempt organizations. Money has been

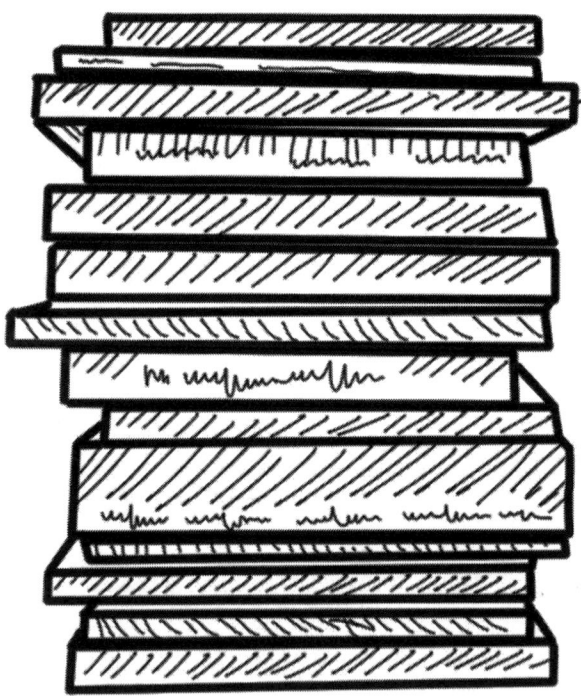

donated to the organization largely by outside donors, whereas a major monetary contribution is made by Donald Trump himself.

His books have served as a major resource for business entrepreneurs and *'Think Big: Make it Happen in Business and In Life'*, was yet another excellent compilation of entrepreneurial guidance. Focusing on maximization of personal and professional achievements, the book teaches you how to back up your opinion aggressively, regardless of what critics say. Following this, some of his other books became famous worldwide, including *'Think Like a Champion: An Informal Education in Business and Life'*, *'Trump 101: The*

Way to Success', *'Trump: How to Get Rich'* and *'Trump: Surviving at the Top'*. Altogether, Donald Trump has authored over fifteen books that have turned out to be bestsellers, with *'Art of the Deal'* being the one of the most successful business books of all time.

Chapter 6
Trump's Political Ambitions

Since the production of the NBC reality series, 'The Apprentice', Trump had become very popular and he took advantage of his fame to enter politics at the right time. In 1999, he switched his voter registration from Republican to the Reform Party and established a presidential exploratory committee for its nomination. However, he left

the party in 2001 and didn't run for president at that time, but he did set forth political views at public platforms.

Trump's party affiliation has changed over the years. Although his party affiliation prior to 1987 is unclear, Trump was an early supporter of Republican Ronald Reagan for United States President in the late 1970s. By 1987, he was identified as a Republican. Later he joined the Republican Party and in 2012 his association with politics resumed, when he publicly announced he was considering running for president again. But

his prior association with the 'Birther' movement, (a group that believed that President Barack Obama was not born in the United States) seemed to have affected his political reputation. Trump had been expressing doubts about the validity of Obama's birth place in the media, which eventually lead Obama into releasing his birth certificate for verification. However, he still did not seem very satisfied and continued to question his origin as well as a variety of his policies.

He was a Democrat from 2001 to 2008, but in 2008 he endorsed Republican John McCain for President. In 2009, he officially changed his party registration to Republican Party, where he has pledged to stay. He has been registered with the party ever since, except for the five months in which he remained Independent, from December 2011 to April 2012.

Trump's political stance is often referred to as 'Trumpism', particularly his views against the free trade and immigrants.

Trump has been described as a non-interventionist and nationalist. He advocates the 'America First' foreign policy and believes in spending on United States military defence. During the start of his political career he revised and reversed his political stances various times on progressive taxation, abortion and government involvement in health care.

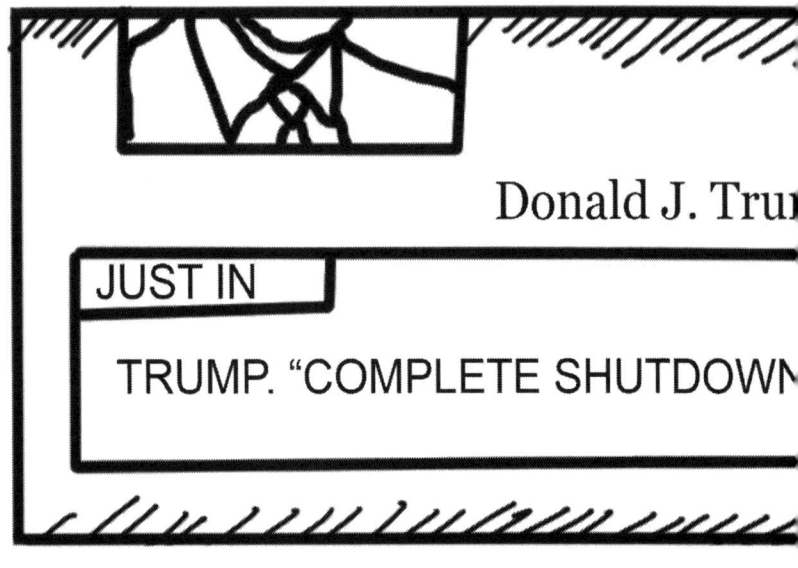

His ideas are often considered rigid and contradictory. He's strictly against opening doors to Syrian immigrants, as he believes it would mean welcoming ISIS to the U.S (a militant group that follows the fundamentalist Sunni Islam) and believes in the restoration of ultraconservative, pure monotheistic worship. As a result of which, he vowed to change immigration laws all over, be it for Muslims or people of any other religion.

Immigration is one of Trump's major concerns, and remains a hot topic of discussion every time his political ideas are considered. He asserts that the Fourteenth Amendment (which states that anyone not born on the U.S soil is automatically an immigrant) does not apply to children of illegal immigrants. However, the topic is still under discussion at the Supreme Court.

One of the most controversial debates is regarding Mexican border security, which Trump believes poses a threat to the U.S as long as Mexicans have easy access. He has publicly spoken against the Mexicans and believes there is an increase in crime and corruption with every Mexican entering U.S territory.

Similarly, another very controversial proposal by Trump was his original proposal in 2015 for a "total and complete" ban on foreign Muslims entering the United States. However, it did cause great outrage and dislike for him amongst certain groups. The policy statement was later revised and corrected to 'temporary' ban and has a series of exceptions, including one for dignitaries and athletes.

He was still very popular amongst the masses and was supported by millions. This lead to his victory in the presidential elections of 2016 as the GOP candidate.

So what is the GOP? The Republican Party, commonly referred to as the GOP (Grand Old

Party), is one of the two major contemporary political parties in the United States, the other being its historic rival, the Democratic Party. The acronym dates back to 1875, when it meant "Gallant Old Party".

Chapter 7
Trump's Presidential Campaign

On June 16, 2015, Trump made his White House ambitions official when he announced his run for president on the Republican ticket for the 2016 elections, joining a crowded field of more than a dozen major candidates. "I am officially

running for president of the United States," Trump said during his announcement at Trump Towers in New York City, "and we are going to make our country great again." He added with his signature

bravado: "I will be the greatest president that God ever created."

Trump began to clinch his own nomination as the GOP candidate for president. But before taking off with this venture, he had to make peace with Obama in order to attract minority votes. So he issued a statement conceding that President Obama was indeed a U.S born citizen. Ever since the onset of the presidential campaign, Donald

Trump started addressing the controversies he has long been associated with.

Trump was the only candidate who said that he might run as an independent if he didn't get the GOP nomination. Not only is that a difficult path to take, but also an expensive one. Trump was probably the only candidate running who could afford to launch an independent campaign.

While the GOP is supposed to stand for the principles of the Founding Fathers, it can be manipulated by the political establishment that can't stand Trump's conservative views.

A few focal points of Trump's Presidential campaign included strengthening U.S. immigration laws; renegotiating or withdrawing from international trade deals, a more aggressive foreign policy in the Middle East, lowering taxes

and repealing financial and environmental regulations.

Trump's slogan throughout his campaign was "Make America Great Again", which he defined in his book, *Crippled America*, as "restoring a sense of dignity to the White House, and to our country in general". States that were very critical of Trump's victory in the primaries included New Hampshire, Nevada, Florida, New York and Indiana.

The NRA endorsed Trump, and he has voiced opposition to gun-free zones, such as in schools. On social and cultural issues, Trump vowed to nominate judges opposed to abortion and once suggested that women who have abortions should be punished. Trump also stated that while he opposes abortion, he believes there should be exceptions in the case of rape, incest, and risks to the mother's life. He has said that he supports "traditional marriage" and argued that

states should decide whether transgender people should use restrooms corresponding to their gender identity.

In an historic moment, he became the first Republican nominee to mention LGBTQ Americans in an acceptance speech. After speaking about a mass shooting at a gay club in Orlando, Florida, Trump said: "As your President, I will do everything in my power to protect our LGBTQ citizens from the violence and oppression of a hateful foreign ideology."

Following this remark, he received a standing ovation from the crowd in the convention hall. Trump also criticized his Democratic opponent saying: "the legacy of Hillary Clinton: death, destruction, terrorism and weakness."

Trump's disdain for political correctness was seen during his campaign and it proved to be what his supporters liked. Some people viewed him as appealing to racism, a charge that he denied strongly.

Trump's campaign rallies attracted large crowds, as well as public controversy. Some of the events were marked by incidents of violence between Trump supporters and protesters, perceived mistreatment of some journalists, and disruption by a large group of protesters who effectively shut down a big rally in Chicago. He was accused of inciting violence at his rallies.

Chapter 8
The Trump Mansion

There is no doubt that the White House is one of the finest pieces of real estate in the country, but would it be a step down for Donald Trump?

While he could never own the property at 1600 Pennsylvania Avenue, his dream is to live there for the next eight years. However, the question

remains: would the White House be up to the Donald's standards?

As a matter of fact, Trump has already announced plans to renovate the White House. Trump promised to install a new ballroom at the White House during a campaign event in Iowa.

Donald Trump loves gold. That is clear when one looks at his 3 storey-penthouse in the Trump Towers, which was inspired by the Palace of

Versailles. The penthouse has an exquisite view of Central Park and Manhattan.

The Trump Mansion was designed by Angelo Donghia in a Louis XIV style. Immediate neighbours to the Midtown East building are the flagships of Tiffany and Co., Harry Winston, Bergdorf Goodman, and Louis Vuitton.

The mansion, worth $100 million, is wrapped in gold and marble with Greek mythology paintings on the ceilings and it is the epitome of

elegance and perfection. Even the vases, lamps and platters consist of 24 karat gold, which accentuates his choices of art and décor. The apartment has a color scheme of warm neutrals throughout, such as beige, gold, rose and blush. However, the golden color scheme is occasionally broken up with large tropical plants, which may hearken to their Palm Beach residence in Florida.

Donald Trump seems set on having massive spaces inside his properties to welcome and host guests, as well as lavish staircases.

An interesting fact is that the Trump Tower was used as the fictional home of Wayne Enterprises in the movie, The Dark Knight Rises.

Pictures of Donald and Melania's wedding can be seen around the apartment and Melania's office desk is usually decorated with short-stemmed yellow roses.

Donald and Melania's son, Barron, has his own floor at the Trump Tower mansion. As Melania puts it: "He can do whatever he wants there. We let him be creative; let his imagination fly

and do whatever he wants..." When Barron was smaller he started drawing on the walls. Trump encourages his son to grow and develop his imagination, so he is allowed to draw on the walls of his playroom. "He is very creative, if you say to a child no, no, no, where does the creativity go?" Trump says.

The White House is seen as a symbol of American history and tradition and has been occupied by every office holder since John Adams, America's second president.

The White House is about two miles from the Capitol building where the US Congress is held - Trump Tower happens to be over 220 miles away.

Also, if Trump chooses to reside in New York he could greatly disrupt city traffic. New Yorkers already frequently take to social media in frustration, when President Obama's motorcade disrupts the city's busy grid.

Whenever the president travels, roads are blocked, traffic can back up for miles and delays can last for hours, but this would be exacerbated in a crowded city like New York.

One might think that it will not be easy for Trump to leave this mansion to move into the White House early in 2017.

A good thing is that the White House has multiple layers of defense, making it a veritable fortress.

An outer iron fence is reinforced by groups of armed guards at the gates and inside the perimeter.

Snipers are perched atop the building and the windows have bullet-proof glass. Additionally, infrared alarms, lasers, and missiles are all reportedly part of the building's defense system.

Chapter 9
Trump's Success

Donald Trump is successful. No-one doubts that. He is an American media personality, real estate developer, and businessman with a net worth of billions.

One thing to say about Donald Trump, introduced as "businessman' at the Republican presidential debates, is that he is anything but 'unpolitical'.

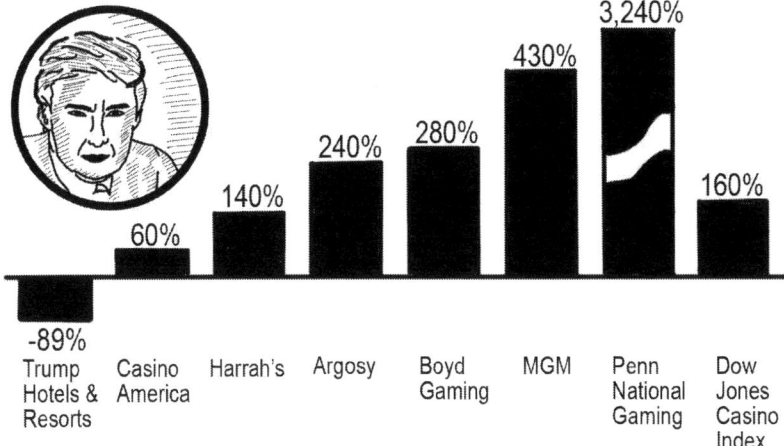

Trump, whose dad was a real estate developer, was involved in politics from childhood. Trump's father, Frederick Christ "Fred" Trump, made a sizable fortune by building and selling housing for American soldiers and their families in World War II. It was at his father's real estate company that Donald got his start in business. In 1971, he took control of his father's apartment rental company, Elizabeth Trump & Son Co., and later on, he renamed it The Trump Organization. Trump stuck mostly with real estate investments during this period, particularly condo associations,

huge apartment buildings and Federal Housing Administration (FHA)-backed housing, all in the New York metropolitan area.

This year was not his first lunge at a presidential campaign either: he ran as a third-party candidate back in 2000. He was more successful 16 years later!

How did he get there? The first thing one can mention is his controversy. He stakes out controversial stands on legitimate issues – like immigration and trade. This brings him enormous news coverage.

Trump is also a celebrity. He is probably the most famous American billionaire. His TV show, The Apprentice, ran for 14 years and he sealed his reputation as a brilliant negotiator and as a result, he has received three times the coverage than all other Republican candidates put together.

The Independent once wrote that Trump speaks at the level of a 4th grade child, which makes it easy to understand his message. And *Psychology Today* wrote: "With terror attacks making headlines across the world, Americans feel uneasy and want to trust someone. Perhaps Mr. Trump's seeming narcissism provides people with the feeling that if he were in charge, someone would know what they're doing — and reduce anxiety."

Another aspect that has helped Trump to be successful, is that he had a ready-made

constituency. During the Obama presidency, Republican voters have been increasingly disenchanted with the party's leaders. They were frustrated when, despite Republican capture of the House of Representatives in 2010, 2012 and 2014 and the Senate in 2014, those leaders were unable to turn campaign promises into laws. Many "constitutional conservatives" simply ignored the fact that the Constitution gives even a narrowly re-elected president a veto on legislation.

Donald tells people what they want to hear. Let's look at a few of his quotes about success from a lifetime in business:

"Remember, there's no such thing as an unrealistic goal - just unrealistic time frames."

"Criticism is easier to take when you realize that the only people who aren't criticized are those who don't take risks."

"I only work with the best."

"Leaders, true leaders, take responsibility for the success of the team, and understand that they must also take responsibility for the failure."

Trump has won the following awards during his life: Liberty, Commandant of the Marine Corps Leadership (2015), Honorary Doctor of Business (2012), Honorary Doctor of Business Administration (2010) and Gaming Hall of Fame (1995).

Trump has simple answers for everything. He is often wrong, but what matters is that he always sounds right. In politics, force of character can be as important as facts (which nobody can agree on anyway). Trump's charisma, his confident and decisive air, forms a huge part of his appeal.

He says things that people have been afraid to say. A lot has been made of Trump's ability to shrug off gaffes. He often makes insensitive or factually wrong statements, that in the past would have torpedoed any other candidate's prospects.

One of the things that are often forgotten, is that Trump has a strong business background and he understands how commerce works. He has more business training than any other American president ever has.

Chapter 10
The Trump Presidency

Trump was elected the 45th president of the United States and in his victory speech at the New York Hilton he promised to focus on economic growth when he would be sworn in the following January. "We have a great economic plan," he said. "We will double our growth and have the strongest economy anywhere in the world."

As president, he will now be tasked with accelerating American economic growth and fixing its problems. Trump has made plenty of enemies along the way as well, including but not limited to fellow GOP contenders Ted Cruz and Jeb Bush, New York Mayor Bill de Blasio, *Fox News* journalist Megyn Kelly, the media in general and even the Pope.

On the campaign trail, Trump admitted the economy wasn't something he looked forward to tackling. And although there is no denying that Trump has done a great job of making himself rich, can he make the rest of America rich too? His immigration plans might cost him a handful of business deals, but they might cost the United States much more too.

The *American Action Forum*, a right-leading policy institute based in Washington D.C. estimates that immediately and fully enforcing

the current immigration law, as Trump suggested, would cost the federal government from $400 billion to $600 billion. It would shrink the labor force by 11 million workers, reduce the real GDP by $1.6 trillion and take 20 years to complete. (Trump said that he could do it in 18 months).

He also outlined some of the details of his vision for health care reforms in America. His 7-point plan calls for the appeal of Obamacare, the allowance of purchases of health insurance across state lines and block-grand Medicaid to states, among other things. The ability for consumers to buy their health insurance in other states is perhaps the biggest health-related proposal Trump has discussed most during his campaign.

Trump's tax plan, which was unveiled in September 2016, is perhaps the most detailed proposal he has put forth yet. It entails implementing tax cuts across the board. It

AMERICAN ACTION FORUM

literally sets forth a scenario in which the lowest earners get to send a form to the IRS reading, "I win". His tax plan is seen as one of the most dynamic and pro-growth tax plans out there.

Trump has also pinpointed imposing tariffs on imported goods, for example, suggesting a 35% tax on automakers that manufacture cars in Mexico. This might bring jobs back to the Unitesd States, or it might not. It could also mean people begin paying more for what they're buying.

After being elected as president, Trump agreed to pay $25 million to settle three lawsuits against Trump University. The deal will keep him from

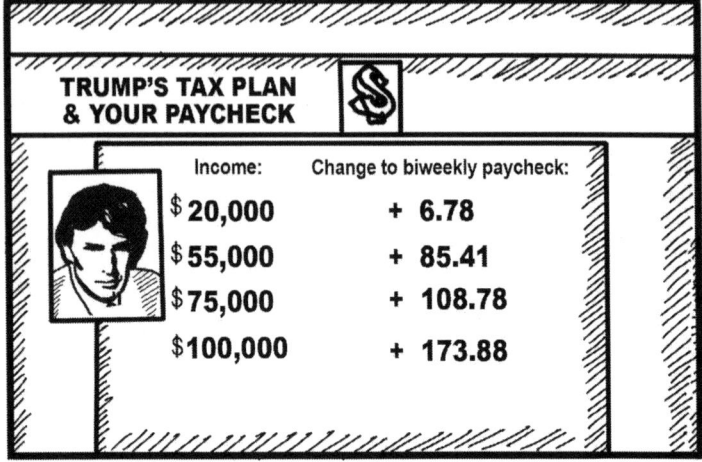

having to testify in a trial in San Diego that was set to begin November 28. The settlement ends a suit brought by New York Attorney General Eric Schneiderman, as well as two class action suits in California. About 6,000 former students are covered by the settlement. The claimants will receive at least half of their money back.

Trump has promised to reduce spending, though he hasn't explicitly said how he is going to do that. Moreover, he has said he will maintain entitlement programs like Social Security and

Medicare, two of the costliest parts of the federal budget.

On November 30, 2016, Trump promised to "remove" himself from his business and says that he will soon announce how he will avoid conflicts of interest when he is president.

Timeline

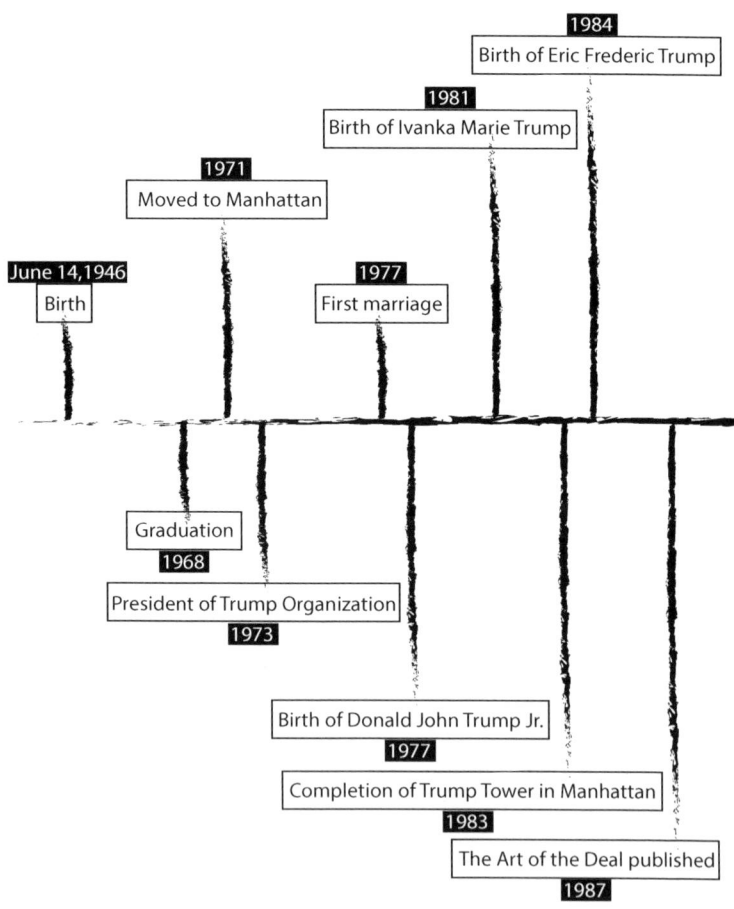

98 | I AM DONALD TRUMP

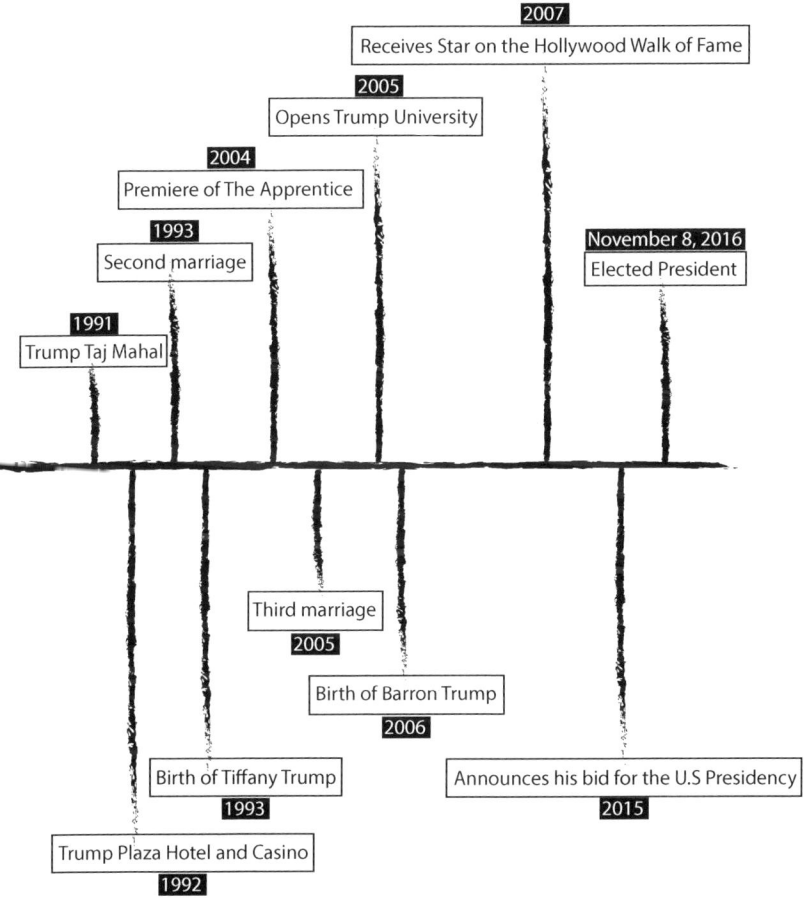

Bibliography

Trump, Donald. *Crippled America: How to Make America Great Again*. New York, NY: Threshold Editions, 2015.

Trump, Donald, and Tony Schwartz. *Trump: The Art of the Deal.* New York: Random House, 1988.

Trump, Donald, and Meredith McIver. *Trump: How to Get Rich.* New York: Ballantine, 2004.

"With Donald Trump As President, Here's What Will Happen To The U.S. Economy". *The Street*. N.p., 2016. Web. 4 Dec. 2016.

Investopedia. "Donald Trump's Success Story." Investopedia. N.P., 2016. Web. 04 Dec 2016.

Schreiber, Barbara. "Donald Trump." *Britannica. com.* Encyclopaedia Britannica, 9 Nov. 2016. Web. 15 November 2016.

Made in the USA
Columbia, SC
02 June 2017